MODERN
POLICE CARS

Robert Genat

Motorbooks International
Publishers & Wholesalers

Dedication

I dedicate this book to my wife, Robin, who gives me the love, understanding, and encouragement to pursue my passions

First published in 1994 by Motorbooks International Publishers & Wholesalers,
PO Box 2, 729 Prospect Avenue, Osceola, WI 54020
USA

© Robert Genat, 1994

Motorbooks International books are also available at discounts in bulk quantity for industrial or sales-promotional use. For details write to Special Sales Manager at the Publisher's address

Library of Congress Cataloging-in-Publication Data

   Genat, Robert.
     Modern police cars / Robert Genat.
      p. cm. — (Enthusiast color series)
     ISBN 0-87938-892-7
     1. Police vehicles—United States. I. Title. II. Series.
   HV7936.V4G45   1994
   629.2'08'83632—dc20   93-48644

On the front cover: *A Ford Crown Victoria of the Ferndale (Michigan) Police Department.*

On the frontispiece page: *Ominous flashing lights in your mirror belong to a 1992 California Highway Patrol Camaro in pursuit.*

On the title page: *1993 Caprice of the Michigan State Police in the department's traditional blue.*

On the back cover: *A California Highway Patrol Camaro.*

Printed in Hong Kong

Contents

Acknowledgments

Without the cooperation of many people there would be no photos and no book. One of the most pleasant aspects of this assignment was meeting law-enforcement officers throughout North America. From big departments to small, there has been one common thread. They are all professionals. So, I have asked them to step forward to take a bow! First Lieutenant Curtis Van Den Berg of the Michigan State Police was a most gracious host. He brought us into his beautiful facility and treated us like royalty. He devoted an entire day from his busy schedule to ensure we got everything we wanted in the way of photos and data. Lieutenant D. W. Miller of the Arizona Department of Public Safety Highway Patrol was quick to respond to my request. He made suggestions for a location, quickly assembled cars, troopers, and a photo car driver so I could get my speed shots. Within the San Diego Sheriff's Department a tip of the hat to Deputies Gene Burch, Roy Frank, Pat Yates, Roger Logan, and a milk bone for Roscoe. Thanks to Lieutenant Forest Billington and his staff of trainers at the San Bernardino EVOC facility for showing me the quick way around their track. Public Affairs Officers John Marinez and Phil Konstantin of the California Highway Patrol gave me access to an unopened stretch of California highway for the photos of their cars. A special thanks to Officer Efrain Quezada, one of CHP's Mexican liaison officers, for the help with the Mexican authorities. Chief Diezel and Sergeant Greg Miller of the Dearborn Police Department gave us unlimited access to their Taurus FFVs. Mexican Federal Police 2DO. Comandante Miguel Cotero was a gracious host to a gringo with a camera. Within the Detroit manufacturers, Bob Hapiak of Chevrolet Division was a superstar. His can-do attitude combined with his knowledge of the police-car market lightened my load considerably. With every silly request I had, he responded quickly. Chevrolet produces a fine police car and that success is due in part to the personal dedication of Bob Hapiak. Ford and Chrysler have superstars of their own. Tom Stevens of Ford, on very short notice, brought us into the X-garage to look at a 1994 Crown Victoria police car and answered all our questions. Frank Mikula and Mike Smith of Chrysler did yeoman's duty getting me the information I needed. Dan Burger, editor of Police magazine, pointed me in the right direction to find the resources I needed. The following get a standing ovation for service above and beyond the call of duty; these guys came in on their days off to help me get the photos I needed: Officer Rick Paap of Seal Beach Police Department, Officer Hugh Daly of the Buffalo Police Department, Officer Tony Mendivil of the Arizona Highway Patrol, Detective Ken Watters of the Ferndale Police Department and Corporal Eric Miller of the Colton Police Department. Each has a great deal of pride in his department. Every department went out of its way to accommodate my schedule and to provide me with the stars of this book, *Modern Police Cars*.

A 1993 CHP Mustang.

Introduction

It usually happens about an hour into the drive. You feel comfortable, the radio volume is just right. The air conditioning has cooled down to a nice level. Yeah, you're twelve over the limit, but no problem! You are alert enough to see any hazard. A glance in your mirror opens your eyes quickly to the kaleidoscope of blue and red flashing lights. Your first thoughts are that they are in pursuit of someone else. Once you see them point to the side of the road it hits you. You've been nabbed. That warm flush of adrenaline hits your face and for some reason the air conditioning isn't cold enough now. You slow down ever so carefully, trying to be an excellent driver now. The uniformed officer is at your right passenger window tapping lightly. You push the down button for the window, and she says, "I just wanted to let you know that your right rear tire looks a little low. There's a service station at the next exit; you may want to have them check it. Drive carefully." You smile and say an automatic thanks. The gods of the road have been merciful today. The phrase "To Serve and Protect" has hit home.

We see them every day. We hope they never stop us, but we want them there when we need them. Law-enforcement officers refer to them as "Units." We know them as "police car," "cruiser," "patrol car," "black-and-white," "squad car," or "cop car." The names are all different, but the car is the same. If we have broken the law it is an ominous foe. If we are in need, it is a dear friend. With its lights, antennas, and push bars it looks rather odd, but it is all functional and all business.

The police car must provide comfort, durability, safety, and performance for the officer. It is as important to him as his weapon. Today's police officer has a difficult job to do and must respond to a variety of situations. These situations make demands on the vehicle that would not normally be made on a passenger car. Today's law-enforcement officer sits in a functional office on wheels. This is their home away from home, a safe haven with radio, computer, and air conditioning.

The life of a police car is not an easy one. It can be scheduled to run three eight-hour shifts a day for 365 days a year in all weather conditions. Each shift may average 100 miles. Within that shift, an officer may get in and out of the car four times or more. A highway patrol shift may put as many as 300 miles on the car. Within each shift there may be periods of idling for an hour or more with all lights and flashers on and air conditioner running. A patrol car may go from idle to full throttle in a matter of seconds. It may run on a city street, paved highway, gravel road, or open field— and along the way jump curbs in pursuit. When asked if he remembered his first high-speed pursuit, one officer said, "No, but I remember the longest. Thirty-two miles at 115 mph." He also confided that it was hard work to drive that fast for that long.

To be able to slow down from high speed is very important to a patrol car. Today's cars are available with ABS braking systems. Initially some departments experienced problems adapting to the sound and feel of an activated ABS system. The manufacturers were quick to jump in with informative videotapes. ABS-equipped cars were loaned to departments for evaluation and training. After seeing the benefits on the test track and in patrol duty, many law-enforcement agencies will not order a car without ABS. The same can be said for air bags. There was a great deal of initial skepticism of the air-bag system, but air bags have proven themselves. Several departments have said that some officers are alive today because of the air bag.

In this book about police cars, I hope to show you what makes the police cruiser different from your passenger car and why. We will take a look at the factory equipment and the aftermarket add-ons. Radar, computers, light bars, and weaponry are all part of today's black-and-white. As you will see, black and white will not always be the color scheme of choice. Color and bold graphics have made their way onto today's police car. We will also take a look at some unique, non-standard police cars currently in service. I have traveled from California to New York and from Canada to Mexico to document the variety of vehicles in use. From ordinary to high-tech, from basic to fully optioned. What I won't show you are undercover cars. Every department asked me not to photograph these cars. If you want to see what they look like just walk out to your garage and look at your car. Undercover cars represent every manufacturer, model, size, and color you can imagine. The more ordinary the better. A large percentage of undercover cars in use are assets seized in drug enforcement arrests. They have well-hidden radios, antennas, sirens, and lights. That car in a parking lot with a child's car seat, a package of disposable diapers and a child's stuffed toy on the floor could possibly be an undercover car.

Today's police cars are the best of the breed. They accelerate faster than any ever built, and they certainly handle and brake better. There are two major police-car evaluations run every year, one by the Los Angeles County Sheriff's Department and one by the Michigan State Police. These departments have been evaluating police vehicles for years and have developed a format to give a civic purchasing agency an excellent set of guidelines to rely on in making a decision. Many of the performance figures quoted in this book are from those tests.

Chapter 1

Henry's Rides
The Ford Cruisers

The blue Ford oval is probably one of the world's most recognizable trademarks. It has been placed on a long line of excellent vehicles that have rolled out of Dearborn, Michigan. Ford Motor Company has, over the years, produced excellent police-car packages.

In 1921, the Detroit police were the first to equip a car with a radio receiver. That car was a Ford Model T touring car. In 1932, Ford released its new flathead V-8 engine. Also in 1932, Ford offered the first "Police Special" option. It was an open phaeton with the new V-8. The new V-8s were popular with the California Highway Patrol, which bought V-8 powered five-window coupes. The flathead V-8 lasted through 1953. It is interesting to note that in the last year of production, the flathead V-8 option was named the "Police Interceptor." The Police Interceptor tag would stay with high-performance Ford engines for quite a few years.

Mustang: No One-Trick Ponies Allowed

In the early 1980s, Ford Motor Company made a move to promote the Mustang as a high-performance police vehicle. An ironic twist of fate positioned the Ford Mustang as a police car. In the early 1980s the California Highway Patrol was evaluating Camaros and Firebirds for their use. The CHP asked the Michigan State Police to include Camaros and Firebirds in its annual police-car evaluation. When Ford Motor Company heard that the GM pony cars were being evaluated, they wanted in. When the day of the evaluation rolled around, only Ford Motor Company was there with a car. The others did not show. The Mustang tested well and was purchased by many departments for highway use. They produced an excellent police package and touted the car as the Porsche catcher. It was a gamble that paid off. The CHP quickly adopted them for their freeway patrols. The nimble little cars had Ford's hot 302 cubic inch engine and heavy-duty suspension. Since the 1970s had produced some of the dullest performing cars ever, the Mustang's performance was a breath of fresh air. The Mustang brought to the forefront the fact that Ford was a player in the high-performance

Though somewhat dated in its aerodynamics, this 1993 Mustang has a classic style all its own. This basic police package has served the CHP for over a decade.

A slick-top Michigan State Police 1993 Mustang waits outside the precision driving facility. Above the special Michigan State Police license plate are two forward-facing red flashing lights.

market again. The public saw a low-cost, high-performance pony car that was being tested under the most rigorous of conditions. The Mustang became the predator and the prey, since many Mustangs with the 302 were being sold to performance-minded consumers. Let's begin our look at the Ford product line with the Mustang.

The 1993 Mustang is the final evolution of a car first in produced in 1979. It was built on the successful, but now somewhat dated, "Fox" platform. Ford has refined it as far as possible. The 1993 model closed the book on Mustang police cars. In 1994 it was replaced by an all new Mustang. Due to the elevated performance levels of the large sedans, the demand for the pony car has dropped. A police package will not be offered on the new Mustang.

The base Mustang offered for police use is the LX sedan version. It has a wheelbase of 100.5 inches and weighs in at 2,834 pounds. It has a driver-side air bag and three-point belts. Fuel capacity is 15.4 gallons of regular unleaded.

The suspension is modified MacPherson struts in the front with variable-rate coil springs. The rear has four-bar-link with quad shocks. Front stabilizer bars are 1.3 inches diameter and rear bars are 0.83 inches diameter. Power front disc and rear drum are standard. ABS braking is not available on the Mustang.

The Mustang is powered by the bulletproof 302 cubic inch engine. It is rated at 205 horsepower at 4,200 rpm with 270 pounds-feet of torque at 3,000 rpm. It has a roller cam, a stainless steel tubular exhaust that produces a wonderful growl and sequential multi-port fuel injection. An EEC-IV electronic engine controls the works. Two transmissions are offered. Standard fare is the five-speed manual driving through a 3.08 Traction-Lok axle. The optional automatic gets a final drive of 2.73, also Traction-Lok.

Many stories have circulated about the CHP and other police Mustangs having monster motors that border on 500 horsepower. Sorry to be the myth-breaker, but no such car has been found. Superchargers have been tested, but the Mustang you see is generally the car they purchased from the dealer.

For the 1993 Mustang, Ford offered the Special Service Package. This package includes a decklid release that was relocated to the left of the steering column. The standard location was in the glove box. Many departments relocated that button to make trunk access faster and easier. An engine oil cooler was added, and if the automatic transmission was ordered, an additional transmission oil cooler was installed. The standard hose clamps were deleted and aircraft-type clamps were installed. The calibrated speedometer has a range from 0 to 160 in 2 mph increments. Tires are Goodyear Eagle GT+4 P215/65R15 on 15x7 cast aluminum wheels. The floor pans are reinforced in the area of the seats for durability. The spare is full size, replacing the small crutch spare. Most departments remove the spare for needed room to mount the radio and siren amplifiers. The balance of the package includes a single-key system and a delete of the sound absorber from under the hood. To date, I have not seen a department that has not ordered the Special Service Package when ordering Mustangs.

Available options are plentiful. The optional seats are heavy-duty, low-back, to replace the higher back sport seats. The low-back seats are upholstered in cloth and have smaller side bolster supports. These smaller bolsters make getting in and out wearing a gun belt easier. The low-back seats are a required option if the Special Service Package is ordered. A 130 amp heavy-duty alternator is available to supply current for the lights, radar, and Mobile Data Terminals (MDTs). Silicone rubber hoses are available. They are green to distinguish them from the standard hoses. They are attached with aircraft-style worm-gear clamps. These hoses are designed for the high-temperature environment of the engine compartment. A drawback is that they cut more easily than the standard hoses, and replacement cost is high. But they are a must if durability is a priority. The side molding on the door is a delete option. This provides a clean door surface for the application of a departmental shield logo. A radio noise suppression package is also available. This adds several copper grounding straps throughout the body. A two-piece speedometer cable is available. This two-piece cable is installed in preparation for the VASCAR time and distance computer. VASCAR is marketed by Traffic Safety Systems of Richmond, Virginia. It has five modes of operation that allow the officer to track the speed of a car without the use of radar. Mustangs have been called "slick tops" because light bars are not usually mounted on the roof. Lack of an adequate roof support structure and a major fouling of the aerodynamic qualities are the reasons.

The end of production of the Mustang police package has been met with mixed emotions. Offi-

A slick-top 1993 CHP Mustang in black-and-white trim. Highway Patrol lettering across the trunk is in gold reflective tape. On the package tray is an assortment of emergency lights. Red and blue are for emergency flashers. The yellow light bar is programmable to provide an arrow to direct traffic to either side of the car. The back surface of the hand-directed spotlights is painted with an anti-glare black paint.

cers have had a love/hate relationship with the Mustang. Its handling has been described as "twitchy" by many, going from a low-speed push to high-speed oversteer. Its legendary performance is now overshadowed by the performance of the Camaro. Without ABS and rear-wheel disc brakes, it's a throwback to the muscle car era. What it has, however, is the awesome reputation as the Porsche catcher. It also has a great reputation for reliability and longevity. Departments that had previously turned in their cars at 60,000 miles have kept their Mustangs for longer because they don't wear out. Speeders may have tried to outrun a standard police sedan, but the Mustang's reputation is legendary. Michigan State Police tests have the 1993 model turning the quarter-mile in 15.22 seconds. It took only 0.34 miles to reach 100 mph. Top speed was recorded at 137 mph. In the all important "catch the speeder range" of 60 to 90 mph acceleration, the Mustang was timed at 8.07 seconds by the Los Angeles County Sheriff's tests. Many departments assign their more mature officers to the Mustang. They tend to have the respect for the machine required for safe and successful pursuits.

Crown Vic: The Full-size Cruiser

Next in the Ford lineup of cars is the LTD Crown Victoria, more commonly called the Crown Vic. This is Ford's best-selling police car. The Crown Vic underwent a cosmetic and mechanical make over for 1992. The new Crown Vic police package was not released until late in the 1992 model run. This is the more aerodynamic car we are now accustomed to seeing on the road.

Many departments still have the pre-1992 model in service, and I feel it only fair to give you some data on it.

While its look is out of sync with today's jelly bean-shaped car, the pre-1991 Crown Vic is a good performer. It came standard with a rather benign 302 rated at 160 horsepower. An optional 351 cubic inch engine was available, upping the horsepower to 180. This engine was not a favorite of the EPA, with mileage ratings of 13 mpg city and 19 mpg highway. This pushed the legal edge of the gas guzzler envelope. Law-enforcement agencies could be given an exemption from the gas guzzler tax by registering with the Internal Revenue Service.

Included with the police package were semi-

Almost docile as it poses for its portrait, the 1993 Mustang's true colors are given away by the 5.0

emblem on the front fender and the bright twin tailpipes.

metallic front disc brakes. These brakes tended to wear fast and squeal. Ford provided a disclaimer on warranty claims involving noise or fast wear. A 140 mph calibrated speedometer with 2 mph increments and a trip odometer were installed. P225/70HR15 speed rated tires were mounted on heavy-duty 15x6.5 wheels with a conventional spare. These tires supported a suspension that had everything beefed up. External oil coolers for the transmission and power steering were also added. The 1990 version was equipped with a standard driver-side air bag. While performance was not stellar, this version of the Crown Vic is still serving well.

It wasn't until 1992 that Ford released a police package for the Crown Vic. Today's Crown Vic is powered by a new 4.6 liter overhead cam V-8. This is an all new engine and Ford's first single overhead cam V-8 since the 1960s. It has aluminum heads with a roller cam, sequential multiport fuel injection and Ford's famous EEC-IV electronic engine controls. When twisted to 4,600 rpm it delivers 210 horsepower and at 3,400 rpm develops 270 pounds-feet of torque. Not bad for 281 cubic inch of displacement. This little powerplant will push the Crown Vic to a top speed of 123 mph. Quarter mile times are in the low seventeens with trap speeds at just over 80 mph. Time for the 60 to 90 mph jaunt is 11.59 seconds. Zero to 100 took 25.5 seconds and 0.48 miles. Not near the times of the Mustang, but respectable for a full-size car. While it has good power, it has excellent EPA fuel numbers of 17 mpg city and 25 mpg highway.

While not giving the officer warp speed, the Crown Vic has other outstanding qualities. Braking is high on any officer's list of demands for a patrol car. The Crown Vic offers excellent four-wheel disc brakes as standard equipment. ABS is optional and integrated with electronic traction assist. Michigan State Police tests had the ABS-equipped Crown Vic stopping from 60 mph in a

1993 CHP Mustang at speed on some of the 99,000 miles of California road over which they have jurisdiction.

distance of 139.6 feet. A non-ABS Crown Vic used 148.8 feet of pavement to come to a halt. Another 10 feet, so who cares? If that 10 feet were a brick wall the driver would care a lot. In addition to shorter braking distances, directional stability under braking is greatly enhanced with ABS. Ford's electronic traction assist is tied into the ABS system. The ABS sensors are used for feedback on which rear wheel may be spinning. The system then applies a modulated braking force to that wheel to reduce the loss of traction. The Traction-Lok rear axle is not available with ABS-equipped cars.

Heavy-duty parts abound with a unique frame and cross member from the standard Crown Vic. The transmission is Ford AOD-E (Automatic Overdrive Electronic). It has a unique tailshaft that is longer than the standard AOD. This is done to shorten the drive shaft. The drive shaft is made out of aluminum. At high speeds the drive shaft begins to flex in a sinusoidal wave pattern. While this minute wave form would never be

San Diego Sheriff's Department 1990 Ford LTD K-9 car with seven-point departmental shield on the door.

Rear windows are tinted extra dark to provide privacy for the dog.

noticed on your passenger car, the engineers at Ford took a long look and determined that with the repeated high speeds that police cars attain, this condition could be detrimental to the transmission, rear end, and u-joints. Revised material and shorter length resolved the situation.

What follows is a summary of the available options for law-enforcement use. An auxiliary fuse panel, which is located near the standard fuse panel, provides three direct battery feeds with 20 amp fuses and three ignition-controlled feeds fused at 20 amps each. These additional feeds are for department-added accessories such as radios and lights. This panel can be used in conjunction with the front wiring option. It feeds a harness through the dash to power front-facing lights.

Additional roof reinforcements are standard and optional. The optional roof reinforcement provides for a roof light of up to 25 pounds. It is made up of a lateral bow crossing between B-pillars and an extension from the windshield header. For roof lights that may be added, a roof wiring harness is available. It provides ten wire leads to the roof. There is an antenna cable option that places a coaxial radio antenna cable in the roof feeding down to the trunk. Spotlamps are available from the factory. They are industry standard 160,000 candle power, A-pillar mounted. If a department wishes to install their own spotlights they can order the spotlight prep package. This includes holes drilled in the A-pillar and necessary wiring. An interesting point is that even though the A-pil-

With the shotgun standing vertically between the front seats, this 1990 Crown Victoria from the San Diego Sheriff's Department is ready for duty.

lars are drilled and could possibly be weakened, the cars pass all required federal frontal crash standards. They are crash tested as they would be configured for sale on the retail market. There is a misconception that police cars are not required to meet federal standards; however, they must meet federal auto standards or they cannot be sold. Also optional are the small "dog dish" type hubcaps. They tend to remain attached during high-speed pursuits and are cheaper to replace if lost. Also optional is the two-piece VASCAR speedometer cable.

Many interior combinations are available for the Crown Vic. Seats are generous, cloth-covered bucket or split bench. The rear seat is available in cloth or easy-to-clean vinyl. A rubber floor mat is an easy-to-clean alternative to carpet. A six-way power seat is available for the driver's seat. This provides additional seat travel for the shorter or smaller driver. An available option is the passenger-side air bag. The mounting of necessary interior police accessories has been complicated by the passenger-side air bag. MDTs, radios, and shotguns all need to be relocated to accommodate air bag deployment.

Taurus: The Bull with a Siren

In the mid-1980s Ford introduced the Taurus. The Taurus was engineered from the ground up on a new platform. It was not a facelift of any previous model. The financial investment was large. The gamble taken was big, but it paid off. It was

Only the push bars break up the clean lines of this 1992 Ford Crown Vic. There's no mistaking this car for an emergency vehicle from any angle.

Right
Black-and-white 1993 Crown Victoria of the CHP. It has a full complement of roof-mounted lights, including the yellow light stick.

A colorful Royal Canadian Mounted Police 1992 Crown Victoria. Tape stripes in blue, gold, and red highlight the beautiful RCMP badge on the door. On the rear quarter panel is an outline of an RCMP horse and rider. RCMP/93-209

an award-winning design that has gone on to be the best selling car in America. It is contemporary, yet familiar.

Ford did not introduce a police package for the Taurus until 1989. Traditionally, police agencies prefer rear-wheel drive cars. Many officers claim that front-wheel drive cars understeer excessively while others claim that they swap ends unexpectedly. I guess they haven't driven a Taurus lately. While many may think that the Taurus SHO suspension was the starting point for the police package, it was actually the other way around. The SHO suspension was a derivative of the police suspension. Like the Crown Vic, Ford added four-wheel disc brakes as standard equipment and ABS as optional. Stopping distances, with ABS, from 60 mph are a respectable 154 feet.

Only one engine and transmission are available for the police-package Taurus, the 3.8L V-6. It produces 160 horsepower at 4,400 rpm and 225 pounds-feet of torque at 3,000 rpm. It will reach a top speed of 123 mph in police trim. Time to reach 100 mph from a standing start is 30 seconds.

A line-up of freshly manufactured Ford Crown Victorias. Painted in a basic black-and-white paint scheme, they await tape graphics and electronic equipment. This group of cars has been ordered with the small "dog dish" hub caps. Many departments prefer the small hub caps over the large ones, which can turn into Frisbees during high-speed pursuits.

Following pages
Fifty years of technological advances separate these two Detroit police cars. The fully restored 1940 Ford Deluxe sedan was the first Ford with hydraulic brakes. The Crown Victoria's hydraulic brakes are four-wheel disc with ABS. Ford Motor Company

This 1993 Ford police-package Taurus of the Arizona Highway Patrol looks like any other Taurus with its full hubcaps and lack of dramatic graphics. The shield on the door identifies this car as belonging to the Arizona Department of Public Safety to which the Highway Patrol is assigned.

Many officers claim that front-wheel drive cars understeer excessively while others claim that they swap ends unexpectedly. I guess they haven't driven a Taurus lately.

Right
Arizona Highway Patrol 1993 Taurus in standard white paint with dark tinted windows. Two radio antennas are seen, one on the roof and the other on the deck lid.

The popular resort city of Hot Springs, Arkansas, recently brought the Ford Taurus into their department's fleet. The Taurus was selected for its better fuel mileage.

Right
A 1993 Taurus coming at you with all emergency lights ablaze. The unit number is displayed in the speaker cover at the center of the light bar.

While many may think that the Taurus SHO suspension was the starting point for the police package, it was actually the other way around. The SHO suspension was a derivative of the police suspension.

Chapter 2

Mopar To Ya

The Chrysler Cop Cars

Years ago, Chrysler Corporation was the major supplier of police vehicles. The cars were big and strong. With the performance of their 440 engine, they were the class of the field. Chrysler last built a police-package passenger car in 1989 with the Plymouth Fury and Dodge Diplomat, more affectionately called the "Dip." Today the only police package offered domestically by Chrysler is on the Jeep Cherokee. Chrysler of Mexico builds a one-of-a-kind police car for the Mexican Federal Police. We will look at these three cars.

The "Dip" and The Fury

The Dodge Diplomat and Plymouth Grand Fury were first introduced in 1981 and were very good selling police cars. They provided an excellent value for the low cost of between ten and eleven thousand dollars. They were the first police cars to offer an optional air bag in their 1988 and 1989 models. These cars were built on the "M" platform. The Dip and Fury looked the same as they ambled down the assembly line. There was no way of telling them apart until the final trim and emblems were installed, identifying them.

Over their lifetime they were built in three different plants: Canada; St. Louis, Missouri; and Kenosha, Wisconsin.

The last three years of production were in Kenosha. During the first two years in Kenosha, vehicles were built under contract by American Motors employees. The final year of production took place after Chrysler had purchased American Motors. The Kenosha cars were the only ones built with the "E" coat body dip process. By the time Diplomat and Fury production moved to Kenosha, much of the tooling for these cars had worn out and had to be replaced. With new tooling to tighten up tolerances, and with engineering improvements, the Kenosha cars were felt to be the best of the line.

The Diplomat and Fury were only offered in a

A-bodied Chrysler Spirit of the Mexican Federal Police. This car is manufactured by Chrysler of Mexico with the optional police package. Behind the shield on the door is an optional bulletproof panel. Wheels are heavy-duty 15 inch five-bolt. It is powered by a 2.5 liter turbocharged four-cylinder engine. Push bars are a factory option.

four-door sedan configuration. There were two police versions available, a city car with a two-barrel carburetor and a four-barrel highway version. The city police car was the same as the taxi with the exception of the high-performance tires on the police version. The body structure was a continual evolution of increasing strength. As each new problem area was identified, it was reworked and reinforced to meet the rigors of heavy-duty service. One sure way to spot an old "M" body police car or taxi is to open the rear door and look for an additional welded reinforcement around the striker. This was one of the many structural improvements made over the years. It was this strong body and stout drive train that endeared it to large city departments. Both New York City and Detroit were big customers of Chrysler. They admired the strength and durability of the "M" body. If the front suspension was damaged in a pothole, department mechanics would just crank on the torsion bars to level it out and send it out on the next shift. Removal and replacement of components was easy. In New York City's bid for cars, they asked for many spare parts. Not small items like spark plugs or hub caps, they wanted fully assembled and painted doors, fenders, and hoods. If any component was damaged, they wanted to be able to pull one out of storage and replace it quick-

A veteran Buffalo Police Department 1989 Diplomat from the traffic division. It is not unusual to see city patrol cars with dents, especially in the northern areas of the country where winter weather is severe.

Crisp looking blue-over-white 1989 Plymouth Grand Fury of the Seattle Police Department, parked in front of their North Precinct headquarters. Chrysler had *over twenty shades of white paint used for police departments' paint schemes. Bill Osborne*

ly. Rumor has it that many of New York's officers, being city dwellers, had never obtained a driver's license prior to being sworn in. Since some had very little driving experience, they tended to damage a lot of cars. Building fully assembled components was an unusual task for Chrysler. As cars are manufactured, the bodies are fully assembled prior to being painted. After paint, the door glass, mechanisms, and trim are installed. To provide New York City with fully assembled doors, Chrysler had to run a special assembly line after hours to do a custom build of those components. The New York cars were painted a unique blue known as "Pepsi" blue. Chrysler would paint a police car any color with a minimum order of five cars, and they did some unique two-tone combinations. There were two dozen different two-tone paint patterns available.

The Dips and Furys do not have stellar performance by today's standards. The city car with the 318 cubic inch engine was topped with a two-barrel carburetor that produced 140 horsepower. It was mated to the large A727 heavy-duty Torqueflight automatic transmission to withstand the rigors of city driving. The four-barrel version of the 318 engine was rated at 175 horsepower and was mated to the smaller A999 Torqueflight transmission. The A999 transmission had a lockup converter and provided better highway mileage. Quarter-mile times were in the high eighteens with the four-barrel-carb version of the 318, and into the twenty-second range for the two-barrel-carb version. Top speed attained was 120 mph in the four-barrel version which, with the exception of the Mustang, was the fastest police car in 1989. Braking was accomplished with a combination of front

disc and rear drum and was rated the best of its day. Wheels were 15x7 steel construction with P215/70 high-performance tires. The only exception to the 15 inches wheels were several cars delivered in Northern California. They were equipped with the smaller 14 inches wheels to accommodate chains for the snowy Sierras. One of the interesting options available was a manual-locking fast idle control. This was installed to allow long periods of idling and to keep the engine charging-system producing enough power to operate the air conditioner, radios, and emergency lights.

Today these wonderful little sedans are being replaced by fuel-injected, ABS-braked, aerodynamic, computerized sleds. The old Dips and Furys are being turned into taxis or purchased for restoration by collectors.

A Spirit with Salsa

While production of traditional police cars has ceased domestically, Chrysler is still producing police-package vehicles in Mexico. The Federal Police in Mexico drive A-body Spirits manufactured in Mexico. The Federal Police are responsible for policing the Mexican federal highway system, a job similar to that of our state highway patrol departments. These are not "econo boxes" with a light bar. They are specifically designed and built for police work. The four-cylinder 2.5 liter engine is turbocharged and drives through a three-speed transaxle. The suspension is heavy-duty and it mounts special five-bolt (four-bolt are standard) 15x6 wheels wrapped with 195/60 high-performance tires. Brakes are four-wheel power disc. The Federal Police cars do not have partitions installed between the seats. Instead they have a special support to accommodate cuffed hands. It

Left
Tough, durable, and low cost, the Diplomat has been a long-time favorite of police departments.

is a steel eye-bolt attached through the floor. It is located on the rear floor area where your heels would be in a normal sitting position. It is very effective in restraining prisoners. The most unusual feature of these cars is the bulletproof shield built into each front door. An option not found on any other production car. Shotguns are not part of their standard police-car equipment. The Mexican authorities carry a Belgian-made, folding-stock assault rifle. There is no mount for it, it just rests between the driver's bucket seat and the center tunnel. Although I was unable to obtain performance specs on this vehicle, I was told by the officers who drive them that they are very satisfied with the performance of this package.

Jeep Cherokee: Police Sport-Utility

Chrysler's only offering for today's domestic police-car market is the Jeep Cherokee. This rugged sport utility has quickly gained acceptance since the release of its police package two years ago. Visibility is excellent due to the thin roof pillars and tall posture. It is available in both two- and four-wheel drive versions. The Police Special Service Package option includes: anti-lock brakes, an engine cooling package with transmission cooler, a 120 mph certified speedometer, a manually controlled extended idle switch, heavy-duty suspension, and heavy-duty seats. The shifter is relocated from the floor to a column mount, making room for radios. It is powered by a multi-port fuel-injected 242 cubic inch inline six. This little engine produces 190 horsepower and 225 pounds-feet of torque. In 0 to 60 tests, it eclipsed the times of several standard police sedan offerings. Because of its lack of spiffy aerodynamics, it suffers at the higher speeds. It still has enough power to reach a top speed of 115 mph. In all honesty, this is not designed to be a highway patrol vehicle. With its excellent ground clearance and skid plates, it is more at home foraging where there are no roads.

33

The most unusual feature of these cars is the bulletproof shield built into each front door. An option not found on any other production car.

This black-and-white paint scheme is the same on all Mexican Federal Police cars. The number of the unit is marked on the sides and on top with large numerals. License plates also carry the number of the unit. Light bars and radios are typical of any US patrol car.

A Michigan State Police K-9 Jeep Cherokee. The unusual hood ornament is standard on all Michigan State Police vehicles.

Left
The license plate identifies it as Michigan State Police Jeep Cherokee K-9 vehicle. One long whip antenna is located on the right quarter panel and two others on the roof. On the roof, behind the rotary beacon, is an air vent for the dog. A small electric fan inside the vent keeps air circulating.

Following pages
A USMC Military Police Jeep Cherokee parks in front of the enormous jet intake of a Harrier. Four-wheel-drive military-police vehicles are needed to patrol the fenced boundaries of military bases. This Cherokee has only one red stripe down the side and a small shield on the door. Red and blue emergency flashers are mounted on the front bumper.

Cop Cars With a Bow Tie
The Chevrolet Cruisers

Chevrolet has long been recognized as the builder of fine high-performance cars. From the fuel-injected small blocks of 1957 to the new ZR1, performance on the track and on the street has endeared people to the bow-tie breed. Back in the 1960s it was not unusual to see a police car with a 409 or 396 engine. Although most were powered by the small block, the big-block V-8s had their share of sales to the police department with a need for speed. Thirty years ago, police packages consisted of heavy-duty front and rear springs and shocks, larger brakes, and 15 inch wheels and tires. All this for a bargain list price of $65. These packages were offered only on the least expensive body styles with minimum comfort or convenience options. It should be noted that the taxi package was identical in content and price. Chevy police cars have come a long way in thirty years.

Chiseled-Edged Caprice

On our roads today, many departments still have the Caprice of the late 1980s in service that was last produced in 1990. It was as boxy as its counterpart of the era, the Ford LTD. It had

evolved as far as it could, but was still a formidable package. Before taking a look at the newer Caprice, here are some numbers and facts on the 1990 model. It had an overall length of 212.2 inches, a wheel base of 116 inches, and weighed in at a little over 3,800 pounds. It was offered with two versions of the small-block V-8 engine and one V-6, all backed by automatic transmissions with lock-up torque converters and overdrive.

The throttle-body-injected V-6 version was rated at 140 horsepower and was intended for city use. Elapsed time to reach 100 mph was a slow 53.09 seconds. Its top speed was reasonably good at 110 mph, considering the size of the engine and relatively poor aerodynamics. It was the slowest of all police models tested in 1990. The good news was EPA numbers of 19 mpg city and 27 mpg highway.

The next step up in the food chain of motors was the 305 cubic inch small block. It produced

Basic police package, this 1993 Caprice awaits markings and lights. A-pillars mount factory spotlights and package tray has two rear-facing red emergency lights.

170 horsepower with 225 pounds-feet of torque. Elapsed time to reach 100 mph was 42.6 seconds, with a top speed of 113 mph. It was an adequate performer at home, on the highway or in the city.

The most powerful V-8 offered was the 350/5.7ltr at 190 horsepower. It only took 30 seconds to reach 100 mph, with a top speed of 122 mph. It tested as the fastest full-size patrol car in 1990. Although GM has an open door policy for anyone wanting to buy a police package, a disclaimer existed that the 5.7l engine was to be sold primarily for law-enforcement or firefighting purposes. Brakes were non-ABS, but the combination of disc and drum brought the Caprice to a halt in

less distance than its full-sized competitors.

The Caprice was offered with the SEO 9C1 police option. This option gave the customer the heavy-duty frame and cross members, 15x7 wheels, heavy-duty suspension and cooling system, heavy-duty brakes with semi-metallic linings, a switch that cuts off the air conditioner at full throttle, and a horn/siren circuit connection. Additional options included holes in the roof in specific locations to run power to a light bar. Multiple options were available for wiring and lighting. One of the more interesting options was the 6F8 option offering additional front door mounted ashtrays. With the standard mounting of radios and

The Chevrolet 5.7 liter, 210 horsepower engine of a 1993 Caprice. The radiator and heater hoses are green denoting that they are the silicone type offered on the *police package. The ABS sensor is located below heavy-duty alternator.*

sirens, access to the ashtray mounted in the instrument panel was impossible.

Seed-Shaped Speedster: The New Caprice

Chevrolet introduced a new body style in 1991. It was curvy and smooth. It has been referred to as seed shaped or the "M&M" in reference to the shape of the candy. The improved aerodynamics were evident in the top speed attained. With virtually the same drivetrain used in the previous year's boxy style Caprice, the new 1991 body style picked up 8 mph in top speed.

Many officers complained that they couldn't see the edge of the fenders like they could with the older boxy Caprices, and that it was hard to handle in close areas. But as they drove it, they became believers that Chevrolet had been listening and was building a car to meet their needs. A full police-package station wagon is available as well as the sedan. The quarter panels for the 1993 model were redesigned to provide a radiused rear wheel opening. This move was applauded by every police-car maintenance department, as it was almost impossible to remove the rear tires while the car was on a hoist. Beginning with the 1991 model, the Caprice represents one of the best overall police cars ever made.

Powering the Caprice is the time-proven small-block V-8 engine. It is available in two versions: the 305 cubic inch with a horsepower rating of 170, and the 350 rated at 205 horsepower. This engine option gives the purchasing agent for a large city the opportunity to buy a lower horsepower car for city street patrol, providing better mileage and reduced gasoline consumption. The same city may opt for V-8-powered cars to patrol its freeway network. The 205 horsepower 350 will go from 0 to 60 in a respectable 8.77 seconds, with a top speed of 132 mph, the best of the large sedans tested.

Braking is handled by semi-metallic linings in a combination of front discs and rear drum brakes

The instrument panel on the new Caprice sports a digital certified speedometer and analog gauge set. A strategically placed placard reminds officer to use overdrive during high-speed pursuit.

with ABS available. The Caprice tips the scales at a little over 4,000 pounds, but will stop from 60 mph in 144 feet thanks to ABS and P225/70 HR-15 tires on 7 inch wide steel wheels (P235/70 HR15 are available as an option).

Chevrolet's Caprice police package offers some very interesting standard items. The speedometer is digital, certified in 1 mph increments. With this speedometer, it is very easy for the officer to pace a speeder and get an accurate speed reading. The readout is from zero to 199 mph. The rest of the gauges (tach, oil, volts, and temp) are analog. There is an automatic cut-off switch for the air conditioner for those full-throttle pursuits. Everything is heavy-duty. The cooling system has dual electric fans. There are external coolers for power steering and engine oil. The alternator is rated at 140 amps output to run all the added electronic hardware. The transmission has been tweaked and has a low-gear blockout to prevent manual downshift. Radiator and heater hoses are silicone with worm gear clamps. The drive-

Two K-9 cars, both Chevrolet Caprices. A 1991 station wagon from the Livonia (Michigan) Police Department and a 1993 sedan from the Ann Arbor (Michigan) Police Department. Both cars display departmental graphics and tinted rear windows to keep inquisitive eyes out of the canine's area. The station wagon's light bar has four white forward-facing "take-down" lights and a siren speaker mounted in the center. The sedan has a new V-shaped aerodynamic light bar with domes in blue, red, and white.

shaft is specially balanced to prevent high-speed vibrations.

Chevrolet offers, by count, more options for a police car than any manufacturer. The buyer can customize cars with every possible combination of after-market toys and have the wiring or mount available. For 1994, with the addition of the 260 horsepower LT1 engine, the Caprice police package will become the fastest full-size four-door sedan ever built, eclipsing the 440 Mopar's legendary performance.

Increased Heartbeat: The Camaro

In response to Ford's success with the Mustang police package, Chevrolet countered in 1991 and 1992 with their pony car, the Camaro. They packaged their small-block V-8s into what they called B4C Special Service Package Camaro. Essentially it's a Z28 in sheep's clothing. Instead of the Z28 emblems, it has the body trim of the RS version. It was available with two versions of the small-block engine. The 305 cubic inch model was fuel injected and rated at 230 horsepower. The 350 cubic inch version, also fuel injected, was rated at 245 horsepower. Both were available with manual or automatic transmissions. The brakes offered on this car, though not ABS, were excellent. With disc brakes front and rear, the 3,400 pound Camaro came to a halt in under 160 feet.

The charter of this vehicle in any agency is

Parked in front of an F-5 fighter aircraft, this 1990 Chevrolet Caprice police-package sedan is assigned to the USMC provost marshal, Marine Corps Air Base, Yuma, Arizona. Simply marked with red and gold stripes, this car patrols the streets and aircraft ramps of the base. It is equipped like any standard police car, with lights, siren, and radios.

simple—enforce traffic laws! Its acceleration and top speed are the best of any police car ever tested. Michigan State Police tests have clocked the 1991 Camaro at 150 mph and the 1992 model at 152 mph. Zero to 100 times are 2.5 seconds less than the 302 powered Mustang. To say it's fast is an understatement. One of the performance features a law-enforcement officer needs in a car is acceleration. Many highway traffic stops begin from a standing start or with a u-turn. Acceleration in these situations is of utmost importance. A speeding vehicle passing a standing officer at 90 mph will be traveling at over 117 feet per second. In eleven seconds they will be a quarter of a mile away. The need to accelerate quickly and attain a speed to overtake the violator is essential. If a patrol vehicle can only reach a top speed of 110 mph, it will take a long time to catch and overtake that 90 mph violator. The shorter the pursuit, the

This Ontario (Canada) Provincial Police Chevrolet Caprice is assigned to highway patrol duty. The light bar is unique and almost looks homemade with its red rotating beacon, fixed mount red and white lights, and two large speaker enclosures. This unit features an interesting set of very large mud flaps and also has a bumper hitch for towing a police boat. An 800 number is displayed for emergency calls.

safer. If a violator feels he has an edge over the officer, he may try to outrun him. That means a long, drawn out, dangerous high-speed chase.

The 1993 Camaro was redesigned with knock-out styling. The sensational exterior is attached to a Saturn-like steel space frame. The wheel base is 101.1 inches, the same as the previous model. The

1993 Caprice of the Michigan State Police in their characteristic and traditional blue. Two other items of longstanding tradition are the single red rotating flasher and the "Stop State Police" lighted hood ornament. TD31 license plate denotes that this car is assigned to the training division.

front suspension has been redesigned using unequal length A-arms. The rear axle is solid with two trailing links and two lateral links supported by coil springs. The Camaro's brakes were already world class and are now even better with ABS. In the Michigan State Police tests, the 1993 Camaro stopped from 60 mph in 128 feet, the best of any car tested.

With the deceleration in hand, the Chevrolet engineers raised the bar on high-performance engines by installing the LT1 Corvette engine. This 350 cubic inch engine generates 275 horsepower at 5,000 rpm. It is available with a six-speed manual transmission or a four-speed automatic. The manual version drives through a 3.42 limited-slip rear end; the automatic has a 3.23 limited-slip. Tires are "Z" rated P245/50R16 on aluminum wheels.

Rear view of Michigan State Police Caprice. A long whip antenna is attached to quarter panel. The front door molding has been deleted and the departmental shield and lightning bolt added to the door.

45

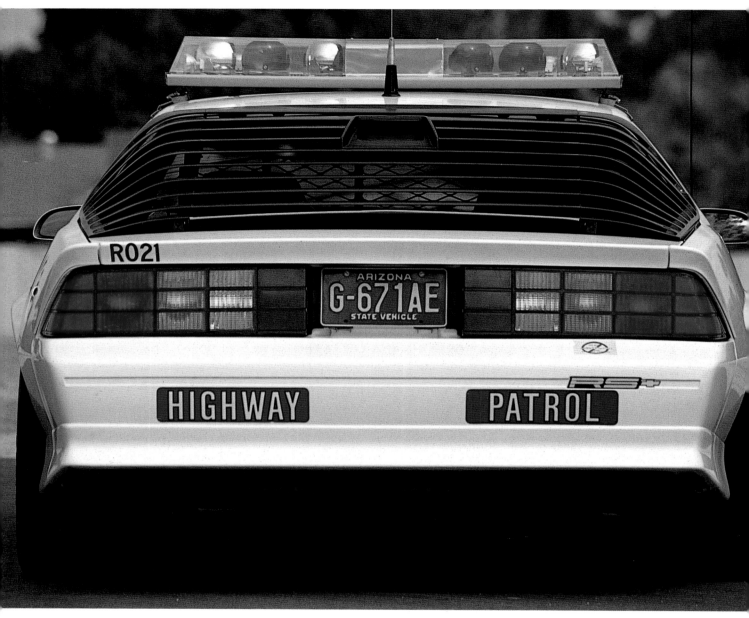

Previous pages
Two for the price of one. A mirror image of a 1993 Michigan State Police Caprice on the wet skid pad of the precision driving facility. This side view shows off the Caprice's aerodynamic shape, which gives the car a low 0.34 coefficient of drag.

Louvers over the hatchback window on this 1992 Arizona Highway Patrol Camaro help keep out the brutal Arizona sun.

48

The clean, unpretentious look of this 1992 Camaro belie its performance capability. Top speeds of 150 mph are easily attained with the 245 horsepower V-8 engine.

The police option is called Special Service Package B4C. It provides the heavy-duty oil coolers and alternator that provide 50 amps at idle. This is an amazing package, well suited for highway patrol use.

Any attempt to place a prisoner in the back seat would be considered cruel and unusual punishment! If prisoners are taken and must be transported, they ride up front and are required to be well behaved.

It is not unusual for an officer in a Camaro to get a friendly wave or a thumbs-up from a motorist. One officer said that while he was ticketing a motorist he was asked by the motorist if he could go back and look at his Camaro. Young people are drawn to this type of car. They will come over to look at the car and ask the officer questions about it. The most frequently asked questions include: How fast will it go? How fast have you had it? Can I borrow it? This type of vehicle

In front of the district headquarters of the Arizona Department of Public Safety, this 1992 Camaro awaits patrol duty. Tinted windows are standard on Arizona's highway patrol cars. Behind its 16 inch alloy wheels and Goodyear 245/50ZR tires are four-wheel disc brakes.

A 1992 CHP Camaro at speed on a California freeway.

brings a new perspective to law enforcement. Young people approach police instead of run away. One Los Angeles-area department has reas-

Left
An aerodynamically shaped light bar with red and blue lights and rear-facing yellow programmable light stick are mounted on the roof of this CHP Camaro.

signed its Camaro to school patrol from the freeways because of the positive interest it generates. Probably one of the best investments a community can make is in a dual purpose car like the Camaro. This car sends a different message than the traditional police sedan. Not only can it patrol the streets, but it can often bridge the gap between the youth of the community and law enforcement.

Belen Middle School
Media Center

A smart-looking 1993 Camaro BC4 police package as it poses in front of a Chevrolet office building. The car's new styling and the Corvette LT1 engine make this the ultimate in pursuit cars. Chevrolet Motor Division

Chapter 4

Optional At Extra Cost
The Finishing Touches

As delivered, each police car appears similar to the car you buy at the dealership. While some manufacturers limit the purchase of police-package cars to fleet buyers only, there are models available with the same equipment as police packages, but much more nicely wrapped. The manufacturer provides the car to the department in its most basic form. It includes wiring for the add-ons necessary for police work. The items added and the way they are located and used are as numerous as the police departments themselves. No two departments outfit their cars in exactly the same way.

Let's start with the basics of what each patrol car must have: identification, dispatch radio, siren, and lights. After we cover those essential items, we will look at all the bells and whistles available.

Color and Recognition

Citizens must be able to identify a police car quickly. If someone in a yellow Pontiac pulls next to me on the freeway and motions me over, I won't stop. The person could be an officer or someone who wants to rob me. I'm not taking the chance; I'll drive on. If a black-and-white with red and blue flashing lights and a shield on the door were to motion me over, well needless to say, over I go with all the dignity and patronage I can muster. This is exactly why unmarked undercover cars don't make or attempt to make arrests on the road.

Each patrol car has a door shield that identifies the agency or department to which it is assigned. In many cases, the door shield is similar to the badge the officer wears. If there is no door shield, the word "police" is on the side in very large letters. It may include the city name, as in "Dearborn Police." On the side of most police cars is the reference to the emergency number 911. The rear of the car is marked with the word "police" and may have the city name. All of these markings are interchangeable with "sheriff" or "highway patrol" or whatever agency the car represents. If the vehicle has a special purpose, such as a lieutenant's car

Clearly visible at the end of the light bar are white alley lights. They illuminate 90 degrees to the side of the unit. They are used when patrolling a parking lot, alley, or other situation where additional lateral light is needed.

or a K-9 car, it may be marked accordingly. Each car has a number on it. Numbering schemes can be very simple or very complex and are designed by the local agency to suit its needs. Many departments will have a large number on the roof for identification by an airborne unit.

The latest trend in marking police cars is reflective tape. In the past, police departments would paint their cars with basic graphic designs and shields. This was a time-consuming, expensive task. If the car was damaged, repainting the graphics was a major project. When the time came to take the car out of service, the car had to be repainted. Today, a lot of departments are ordering their cars in a solid color, usually white. Some departments have long-standing traditions of a unique standard color, such as the Michigan State Police and its characteristic blue. After the service life of a patrol car ends, it can be de-striped in a short time with no damage to the paint underneath. This car can now be sold to another department, and they can add their own graphics.

The other advantage of reflective graphics is a high degree of visibility for the officer in pursuit. After doing a ride-along and talking to many officers, a common complaint appears: people just don't see them. Anything enhancing visibility is an asset to the officer. One disadvantage is that they can't hide anymore. Sitting on a side street waiting for someone to run a stop sign is a tough thing to do when you glow in the dark.

Prior to ordering new cars, departments usually

One of the Ferndale Police Department's 1992 beautiful Crown Vics. The graphics are integrated into the aerodynamic lines of the car. This car is highly visible day and night. Clearly and colorfully marked, it is a standout in the law-enforcement community. Red, white, and blue Michigan bicentennial license plate harmonizes well with graphics.

have a meeting at the lieutenant level and above to discuss the look of the department's new cars. The entire design could be done on a napkin over lunch with the chief, or a graphic artist may be called in. Many basic designs have been turned over to graphic artists to refine proportions, make suggestions and actually cut the designs from the reflective tape. Today's more aerodynamic vehicles beg for a more artistic approach to vehicle marking.

One of the most notable designs is the stylized American flag of Michigan's Ferndale Police. Of this design, Captain Michael Kitchen of the Ferndale Police Department said, "With the availability of reflective graphics, we were able to develop a striking and effective design that enhances the identification of this police vehicle." The Ferndale Police Department has carried this design to their uniform patches and to all of their vehicles, including patrol bicycles. The beautiful graphics soften the sometimes hard-edged perception of law enforcement. When shooting the photos of Ferndale's car, a group of children joined us, drawn to the car. The officer helping us began answering questions about the car for the gathering kids—community-based policing at its best!

Ten-Four: Communication

Each police car has a radio for voice communication to the dispatch center. This radio will probably have a second channel, commonly called a tactical channel, to communicate car-to-car. Larger departments may have separate chan-

A 1991 Caprice of the Buffalo Police Department. The gold stripe identifies it as a lieutenant's car from precinct three. Buffalo's regular patrol cars are marked with blue stripes only.

57

Trooper's view from behind the wheel of a 1993 Mustang. Fixed-mount radar points toward the front. Below the radar and its control box is the siren. In the dash are two radios.

nels for mutual aid between neighboring departments, SWAT, surveillance, special events, and administration. Most police voice communication is done VHF low band (30.000-50.000 MHz) and VHF high band (138.000-174.000 MHz). Some cars now have UHF radios that operate in the 406.000-512.000 MHz band. In metropolitan areas where there are many adjacent municipalities, each having its own radio frequency in a possible different band, it may be necessary to have three or more radios for communication in mutual aid situations. Supervisors' cars will probably have the greatest amount of radio equipment. Supervisors may have cellular phones for additional secure communication that will not interfere with normal radio communication. Patrol cars may also be equipped with a CB radio to aid stranded motorists. The way to tell which band of radio is being used is to look at the antenna length. The basic rule is, the longer the antenna the lower the frequency. Cars with the long, whip antenna use VHF low band radio. Each radio has

its own antenna. Radio installation is done by putting the control head within the officer's reach on the dash or on the console. Attached to the control head is a keyable microphone and a speaker. The main radio unit or units are mounted remotely in the trunk. One of the car's antenna may be for a repeater. This would be installed if the officer carries a hand-held remote radio. These hand-held radios do not have enough range to reach the dispatch center, so their broadcast is picked up by their car's repeater and beamed to dispatch from the car's radio antenna. For agencies with a large territory to cover there are fixed base repeaters. These repeaters will take the signal from the remote car and broadcast it back to the communications center. Officers and dispatchers communicate on the radio in their own lexicon. This language consists of codes for events and responses. This form of aural shorthand is used nationwide, but each city may have a different set of codes. APCO (Associated Public-Safety Communications Officers) has a suggested list of standard "ten" codes (ten-4, message received, or ten-7, out of service). Each department or region may have its own expanded list of codes.

Yelp and Wail: Sirens

Within easy reach of the driver, on the dash or console, is a control box for the siren and light bar. These switches may be incorporated into a single box or may be separate. The siren in today's patrol car produces a series of wails and yelps through a speaker that may be mounted in the center of the light bar or somewhere behind the front bumper. This speaker is usually rated at an eardrum-bursting 100 watts. A 200 watt speaker is available for those hearing impaired or about to be! The activation for these sirens can be wired into the car's horn button, or a separate button may be placed on the floor for foot activation during pursuit. These siren and light activation boxes are often called "code 3," the standard police code for use of siren

Reflective tape graphics ignite with a small amount of strobe during the middle of the day. At night this reflectivity enhances the visibility of the cars and adds to the safety of the officers.

and flashers in response. A public address system is incorporated into most siren systems with a dash-mounted microphone.

Rollers and Gumballs: Light Bars

Lights and emergency flashers are a subject unto themselves. Essentially, these lights make the police car highly visible and easy to identify. Thousands of emergency-flasher combinations are possible, from a single roof-mounted rotating bea-con—lovingly nicknamed the "gumball machine"—to rather elaborate light bars some-times called "rollers" because of the rolling action of the multiple lights.

Rotating beacons were first used in the late 1940s, and light bars began to light up the roads in the mid-1960s. The Michigan State Police has tra-ditionally had the single red rotating beacon because the red beacon has always fulfilled its function, so there is no reason to change! The sin-

Illuminated plexiglass hood ornament on Michigan State Police patrol cars. This longstanding tradition dates back to the days when a trooper would pull alongside a car to make an arrest.

gle red beacon increases the aerodynamic drag of the car by only 2 percent, whereas light bars increase drag up to 7 percent. That translates into more performance in the higher speed ranges for cars with the red beacon.

Most fixed-mount rotating beacons contain two to four bulbs and a motor to rotate that assembly in a colored dome providing 360 degree visibility. The average single rotating beacon will output 90 to 105 flashes per minute. There is not much flexibility with the rotating beacon. It is either on or off and provides no color options other than the color of its dome. Multi-functional light bars are today's hot ticket. They provide multi-color displays of high intensity.

The effectiveness of a warning light can be attributed to three things: how much candle power is emitted, how the light is output (strobe, rotating, or constant), and the color of the light. Light output for the individual halogen lights, rotating or constant, in most light bars is in the 50,000 to 70,000 candle power range. Strobes have a much

higher output at 1.5 million candle power for a much shorter duration of about 250 microseconds. Flashing lights are designed to get attention.

The light bar also contains lights (usually white halogen) that can be turned on for constant illumination. At the end of the light bar are mounts for 50 watt white halogen lights. These lights point outboard of the car and are called "alley lights." They are used for patrol of an alley or parking lot where light is needed directly to the side of the police vehicle. The other fixed white lights in a light bar are called "take-down lights." They point toward the front, but can also point to the rear. They are used to illuminate a vehicle that has been stopped or to provide additional light as needed. Another white halogen light incorporated into many light bars is center mounted and provides a forward figure-eight sweep to provide extra illumination in a pursuit situation. The possible combinations of lights are legion, and the latest in light-bar designs provides a more aerodynamic shape to reduce drag while providing multiple light combinations. Each department has researched the many optional light bars available for their specific needs prior to purchase. What may be ideal for a highway patrol unit may not be adequate for a local sheriff's department.

And then there's light color. Humans perceive color in specific ways. We have been conditioned to recognize red and blue flashing lights as belonging to an emergency vehicle. Flashing yellow lights are understood to be caution lights. The reason there are both blue and red lights on police cars is that the human eye is more sensitive to red light during the day and blue light at night. Red lights at night tend to blend into every other red light on the road. It is easier for our eyes to distin-

Traditional single red rotating beacon, affectionately called a "gumball machine," on a 1993 Michigan State Police Caprice.

guish the blue lights at night, thereby getting our attention more effectively. Yellow lights have also made their way onto the police vehicle. Rear-mounted yellow lights are used by some departments to augment red and blue lights. More recently, many departments have adopted a rear-facing "light stick" option that can be programmed to create a repeating sequential pattern of flashing yellow lights to direct traffic in a specific direction. This bar of yellow directional lights may be on the back of a light bar or mounted on the rear package tray.

Some departments have gone to the "slick-top" look. Without the highly visible roof-mounted light bar, they look more stealthy. Some departments believe that the weight and drag of the light bars adversely affect the handling and stability of their police cars. Many Mustangs are "slick top" with a windshield-mounted red light behind the rear-view mirror and blue and red push bar or grille-mounted lights that flash in a wig-wag pattern. Some departments use a colored, hand-directed spotlight for forward recognition. In addition to the add-on lights, headlights and taillights are wired to provide a wig-wag flashing sequence.

More Options: Please Be Seated

Now your police cruiser is outfitted for patrol. Well, not quite. There are a few things we need to add. A 12 gauge shotgun would be nice. Locking mounts are available for the upright position between the front seats. Some departments, on Mustangs and Camaros, mount their shotguns on the lower edge of the driver's door, behind the driver's seat, or in the trunk. The mount needs to be secure for two reasons. A "loose cannon" during a high-speed pursuit would not be in the driver's best interest, and we would not want it to stray

This CHP Camaro carries an aerodynamic light bar. The car's headlights flash in a wig-wag sequence when emergency flashers are activated.

The front of the K-9 car is the same as any patrol car. A console has been built between the seats. In front of that console is the radio, siren, and vertical-mount shotgun. A laptop computer is carried along to do paper work. After returning to the station at the end of each shift, officers can down load and print accumulated data.

into the wrong hands.

To keep those hands off that weapon, most departments have opted for a partition between the front and rear seats. This partition uses up a bit of rear-seat leg room, but most folks riding in back are only along for a short ride. Partitions are made of a heavy gauge tubular metal framework that goes from the rocker sill, around the roof and back down to the other rocker sill, almost like a roll bar. Across the back of the front seat, between the uprights, is a seat protector plate of 14-gauge steel. From the top of the seats to the roof is either a Lexan window (with or without a sliding opening) or the upper portion may be made of expanded metal screen. Bad guys in back, good guys in front.

Something new has been invented for the rear-seat passenger. It is a molded fiberglass seat, offering some specific advantages. First, it makes riding handcuffed in the back seat much more safe and comfortable. When handcuffed, it is very difficult to sit with comfort because the hands are crossed behind the body in the small of the back. This pushes the prisoner about 4 inches forward in a rear compartment already lacking in knee room. The fiberglass seat has indentations to accommodate the prisoner's elbows, arms, and cuffed hands. The prisoner can now sit back in the seat and be properly and comfortably secured with a three-point seat belt and shoulder harness. Sitting back with arms in the cutouts, the prisoners are less likely to slip their cuffs. The single-piece molded fiberglass also prevents hiding or disposal of contraband in the seat. Finally, the fiberglass is easy to clean. For the same reason, many departments order their cars with a vinyl rear seat.

Four-Legged Partner: K-9

The K-9 officer and his canine partner have special needs, so K-9 cars differ from standard police cars. Some departments opt for a station wagon or sport utility to provide a canine seat. Other departments modify an existing patrol car for K-9 use. If it's a standard sedan, they may remove the rear seat and build a platform for the dog to sit on. All of the inside handles and arm rests are removed, since dogs tend to chew on them. An ingenious device has been marketed to provide a quick exit for the dog. The officer has a small remote similar to a car alarm unit. When the button is pushed, one or both of the rear doors will pop open, giving the dog access to his human partner. The door opening is facilitated by a rather large gas spring. Station wagon K-9 cars have a remote to lower the rear window. Extra ventilation and cooling capacity—for the dog and for the car—are often built into the K-9 car because the dog may be left in the car with the air conditioning running for long periods of time while the officer is away from his car. Some departments have cut louvers into the hood, hot rod style, to help with engine cooling. Other vehicles have a small, roof-mounted fan that runs continually. K-9 cars are usually taken home at night by the officer. The officer and the dog are partners off duty as well as on.

Zap: Radar

Radar is a nasty word to those with a mind to

This is where the bad guys sit. This specially constructed fiberglass seat has scallops cut for the arms, elbows, and cuffed hands of a prisoner. This seat prevents the hiding of contraband and secures the prisoner with a three-point belt. The lower portion of the partition is thick steel with a framework that resembles a roll bar. This model has a sliding Lexan window. Some partitions have expanded metal screens. Although the door has an inner handle, it can be opened only from the outside. The floor covering is a black rubber mat.

speed, but it provides law-enforcement personnel a very accurate tool to catch speeding violators. Radar systems can be installed with fixed forward or rearward mounted antennas, or both. These

antennas provide coverage when parallel to or driving in the flow of traffic. Many departments opt for hand-held radar, which enables the officer to sit diagonally to the flow of traffic, such as in a median, checking traffic in both directions. Another advantage of the hand-held unit is that it can be easily transferred from car to car.

Today's radar operates in the K-band, that is 24.15 GHz and is true Doppler radar. Simply defined, Doppler is the measurement of accelerated or decelerated reflected sound waves. We have all heard the sound of a train approaching a crossing. The sound waves from the horn are accelerated to your ear by the speed of the moving train; therefore, you hear a higher frequency. As the train passes you, the frequency shifts to a lower tone, because the sound waves are traveling away from you. The Doppler radar measures that difference and produces an mph readout for the operator.

Today's speed enthusiasts have access to an assortment of detectors and jamming devices. If someone is trying to jam the radar, a code is displayed on the radar readout telling the officer that a jammer is in action, and the officer can nearly always pinpoint the car operating the jammer. Now that car will usually become the target for an extended pace.

The very latest in speed detection is the laser detector. It uses light waves instead of sound waves to catch speeders. Throw away your radar detectors and jammers, because law enforcement can now move at the speed of light. Although laser detectors are available to the consumer, their effectiveness is questionable. The narrow laser beam (2 feet in width at usual detection range) must hit the detector to be recognized. If your detector is on the dash and the laser gun illuminates your front bumper with its narrow beam, your detector will not sense the laser, and you will not know that you have just been nabbed!

The Information Age On Wheels: MDTs

The latest in high-tech police-car equipment is the MDT (Mobile Data Terminal). The MDT system provides the officer on the street direct access to several criminal justice data bases and secure car-to-car communication. One advantage of the system is that the officer accesses the data base directly without any other human intervention. This frees up personnel and shortens access time for information. Access time is short, with a maximum time lag of 15 seconds for a request during busy periods and only a few seconds when there are fewer demands on the system. The system usually comes back with more information than the officer can handle in a short period of time, so a scratch pad is built into the system to hold responses. Officers can make queries by license number or vehicle identification number. Officers can query individuals and their driving record.

MDTs offer car-to-car and car-to-station communication. Communication can be made to all cars on the system if needed. Computer Aided Dispatch (CAD) is available, but most depart-

Deputy Roscoe lies patiently in the back of his specially modified K-9 car. The rear seat has been removed, and a carpeted platform has been built for him. A cut out has been made in the platform for a water dish. A large gas spring pushes the door open when the latch is remotely activated, giving the dog access to the outside world. The partition has an opening door so the dog can stick his head through and get a pat on the head. The rear door handles have been removed, since the dog will tend to chew on them as he already has on the seat. Rear door windows are supplemented with screen to give the dog fresh air while keeping him contained.

Following pages
Deputy Roscoe sits in front of his 1990 Ford Crown Vic K-9 car from the San Diego Sheriff's Department. This attractive green-and-white color scheme is being phased out in favor of black-and-white cars. The C-pillar has a K-9 graphic and a notation on the rear doors that there is a police dog inside and that you should keep your distance.

A well-worn hand-held radar gun sits on the seat of this highway patrol Camaro awaiting another speed violator.

ments still use verbal communication for this function. This communication is sent via 800 MHz frequency on a data stream. This form of transmission is very secure and cannot be intercepted by conventional police scanners.

Another function provided by the MDT is a HAZMAT (hazardous materials) query. Each commercial carrier transporting hazardous materials must display a diamond-shaped placard with a number on it. If there were an accident, the unit responding would simply access the MDT HAZMAT function, enter the numbers from the placard and receive information needed about the materials on board. This data is available to officers by book or by voice communication, but the short access time using the MDT in an emergency situation could be a lifesaver.

The MDT system is very easy to use and training takes less than 2 hours per officer. Today, MDT mounts are elevated on the passenger side of the dash. With newer cars equipped with passenger side air bags, the terminals will need to be relocated. One department has removed the pas-senger seat from its new Camaro and has placed the MDT in that space. Newer MDT models have smaller screens and can be mounted lower in the console area. One company is already marketing a heads-up display (HUD) for patrol cars. It will project the MDT output onto the windshield in front of the officer, much like the HUDs in the latest fighter jets do for their pilots.

Undercover cars can have the functionality of the MDT in a smaller hand-held version, initially called "KDT" (keyboard data terminal), now called "PDT" for personal data terminal. They are about the size of a standard hardcover dictionary and have an LCD display. They are battery powered or can be plugged into the cigarette-lighter socket. Because of restrictions put on hand-held radio equipment, their range is limited.

What's in the Back?

The trunk of today's patrol car is filled with equipment. Trunk room for non-essential storage is limited, since radios and light controllers are permanently mounted there. The trunk may or may not carry a spare tire. Some departments remove the full-size spare and put it in storage to be placed on the vehicle at a later date when a new set of tires is needed. Or it will be used as a spare for a vehicle in need. Other trunk equipment includes: a first aid kit, flashlights, blankets of two types (one to wrap around a cold child and another of yellow plastic to cover an accident victim), a bag with riot or SWAT gear, accident measuring devices, flares, and reflective diamonds or orange cones for accident scene traffic control, rolls of yellow barrier tape for crime scene restraint, personal briefcase filled with extra forms and tickets, a teddy bear for calming a frightened child, a wide leather belt for restraining prisoners who must be transported in the front seat of smaller patrol cars like the Mustang and Camaro, and rain gear for those nasty weather days when folks get into accidents. Supervisors' cars will occasionally carry a camera to document the scene of a fatal accident. Highway patrol cars covering long distances in the warmer climates carry a five-gallon water bottle. Occasionally, the shotgun is carried in the trunk instead of the passenger compartment. Some cars carry a Ruger Mini-14 rifle.

Center-mounted MDT with small screen. Function keys to the right select the desired form. Here, a name query form is waiting to be filled in. Only seconds are needed to get a response.

The rear compartment of a 1992 Camaro of the Arizona Highway Patrol is filled to capacity with necessary items. The gym bag contains SWAT gear, a blue fleece blanket (to warm an accident victim), a yellow plastic blanket (multiple uses), a 5 gallon water bottle, a large leather belt to secure a prisoner in the front passenger seat, and a standard issue state trooper hat.

Chapter 5

Special Delivery

Unique Patrol Cars

Until now, our look at modern police cars has been at the police packages that the factory offers. A standard factory package cannot meet the needs of every department. In this chapter we will look at cars obtained from other sources. Some are seized assets converted to police use. Others have been obtained for a specific use in law enforcement or for community relations. They are all real police cars!

Saleen Mustang—Seal Beach, California

The city of Seal Beach lies at the northern end of Orange County just below Long Beach, California. It is the home of the naval weapons storage facility. The roads that run between the storage areas are long and straight, just right for a little excessive speed. To reduce the speeding on these roads the Seal Beach Police Department has the absolute pit bull of pursuit cars, a Saleen Mustang. In 1989 the Saleen folks decided to build the ultimate patrol car with hopes of selling more. The city of Seal Beach was the first and only recipient of Saleen's craft. It was dubbed SB/S for Seal Beach Special. It is your basic 1989 Saleen Mustang with a few official goodies added. The roll

bar mounts the antennas for the Hawk radar, one pointing forward and one to the rear. The Hawk radar is wired into the cruise control and calibrated speedometer. The roll bar also has a mount for the shotgun behind the bucket seats. The seats are standard Saleen issue Flofit, with a five-point restraint. Being belted in is a serious requirement, because when this pocket rocket takes off, it's with a vengeance. While the engine is stock Ford 5.0 liter issue, the transmission has been warmed over by Art Carr Transmissions of Fountain Valley, California. The final drive is a 3.55:1 Traction-Lok. This limits top speed to something less than a standard issue black-and-white Mustang, but getting there is half the fun and this baby gets there. Providing the grip to the pavement are 16 inches Goodyears on alloy rims. The limit in top speed is not a problem for the type of enforcement this car routinely pulls. As it was explained to me, they don't want to be involved in long, drawn out high-speed pursuits. This car accelerates so fast, in such

The Seal Beach (California) Police Department's everyday, one-of-a-kind patrol car—a 1989 Saleen Mustang.

Don't mess with this black-and-white. Acceleration is outstanding due to a lower rear-end ratio, specially modified transmission, and large Goodyear tires. Its only job is traffic control.

a short time, that they catch the violator before he has a chance to get away. Seal Beach will be selling its Mustang when it reaches the end of its service life. Some lucky collector will snap it up almost as fast as it accelerates.

1984 Corvette—Colton, California

The city of Colton, California, lies at the east end of the Los Angeles basin in San Bernardino County. In addition to the usual collection of black-and-white patrol cars, the Colton Police Department has a 1984 Corvette. This four-wheeled blaster was obtained as seized property in an arrest involving drugs. The previous owner gave it up after a 120 mph pursuit. This car lost in its first race with law enforcement and became a seized asset because of the illegal cargo on board. Since that time, it hasn't lost a pursuit yet.

It is a stock 1984 Corvette. The instrument panel sports aftermarket wood trim. Originally black with silver leather interior, it took only a little white paint on the doors and top to turn this

one-time bad guy car into a traffic and D.A.R.E. car. The radio, sirens, and light bar are standard police-car issue. The ownership of this car has been turned over to the sixty-five-member Colton Police Officers' Association. They have done all of the work on the car and currently maintain it. For this reason, the guys in the department are particular about its duty. It is very popular with kids as the D.A.R.E. car when visiting schools or participating in community events.

1991 300ZX and Infinity Q45—San Bernardino Sheriff's Department EVOC

EVOC stands for Emergency Vehicle Operations Center. It is operated by the San Bernardino Sheriff's Department and is one of the most advanced driver training facilities in the nation. Gone are the days when having reflexes sufficient to catch a set of keys was enough to qualify an officer to drive a police unit. Police departments have come to realize that fender-benders are costly to the department's budget and detrimental to the driver's safety. Many serious accidents are avoidable with proper training. Courses at this facility range from a half-day refresher to a full three-day pursuit program. EVOC conducts its own academy classes and accommodates other departments as well.

The students drive older Ford and Chevy police sedans complete with roll bar. Not very glamorous, but they serve the students well. The instructors drive a range of Nissan products used as "rabbits." Nissan has been kind enough to donate pre-production prototypes and other test cars to the facility. The only catch is that the cars must be destroyed after EVOC is finished using them. The cars come without VIN plates so they can never be licensed or street driven. But the wheels are driven off them at the center. The two cars shown here are adorned with the San Bernardino Sheriff's logo. The Q-45 also has a light bar and radio. The weekend duty for these cars is community relations. They are loaded on a flatbed truck and transported to county events where they attract lots of attention.

1991 T-Bird Super Coupe— Arizona Highway Patrol

You may have seen Ford's T-Bird Super Coupe, but I'm sure you haven't seen one like this. This baby moves! It was loaned to the Arizona Highway Patrol by Ford Motor Company. Ford has had a long association with the Arizona Highway Patrol. Cars are loaned to the department for the purpose of testing specific parts, or in this case, the engine. Ford wanted to know how the supercharged V-6 would perform under heavy use. This is the same car you could have bought in

1991: Thunderbird Super Coupe with the 210 horsepower V-6, a five-speed manual transmission, and ABS braking.

Because of the great distances driven in Arizona, many of the officers are assigned a car that they may even take home at night. Such is the case with the officer assigned to this car. He told me a story of one speeding ticket. While he was parked in a median, a passing vehicle was checked with radar at 110 mph. The vehicle never slowed down as it passed. The officer started his pursuit and paced the vehicle at 120 mph. After pulling the violator over, the officer was told that the driver saw him, but didn't think he could catch him! The excellent acceleration and smooth suspension made this apprehension possible. More than once,

The whale tail on Seal Beach's Saleen Mustang is emblazoned with the word "police." There is no mistaking it for a standard Saleen Mustang. The small white letters, SB/S, in the lower corner of the quarter window stand for Seal Beach Special. Barely visible inside the back window, attached to the roll bar, are two radar antennas, one pointing forward and one rearward.

The 1984 Corvette patrol car owned by the Colton (California) Police Department. The Corvette was seized following a traffic stop where drug contraband was found. It is maintained as a regular patrol car, at no cost to the city, by the Colton Police Officers' Association. Markings between the taillights identify the origin of the car.

after getting a ticket, violators look at the car and say, "Nice car," realizing that they have been nabbed by one of the most unique patrol cars in the country. When asked about problems with the car, the officer said that when he stops to eat or get gas, it attracts a crowd of people wanting to know all about it. He often has a hard time getting away!

Left
The Seal Beach Saleen Mustang offers the driver a stout bucket seat with a five-point harness. The carpet around the gas pedal is well worn, a testament to its use. The radar control box is connected to two antennas to track traffic both ahead and behind. The small remote on the console is for the radar. The red button at the rear of the console is for the Halon fire-extinguisher system.

Camaro IROC-Z— Ohio State Highway Patrol

The Ohio State Highway Patrol has three new IROC-Zs to patrol their roads. The cars were donated to the state by a former "chop-shop" operator specializing in stolen Camaros. Because the cars were assembled with stolen parts, they cannot be legally sold or titled. Instead of sending them to the crusher, the state has put these orphans to good use enforcing the rules of the road. Colonel Thomas W. Rice, superintendent of the patrol said, "Our ultimate goal is to eliminate traffic crash fatalities and injuries in Ohio. We will only be able to achieve this goal through voluntary compliance by the public with motor vehicle laws. We believe that the presence of these cars on our highways will enhance that voluntary compliance." The

A generous donation from the Nissan corporation has given the San Bernardino (California) County Sheriff's Department several high-performance cars to be used

as rabbits on their driver's training course. The Infinity Q45 and 300ZX are marked with the sheriff's department door shield and graphics.

troopers assigned to the Camaros receive additional training in their new cars at the academy in Columbus. The IROC-Zs will be rotated to all of the posts around the state to give all troopers a fair shot at high-profile law enforcement.

Previous pages
Colton's Corvette was originally black, so it was a simple matter to paint the doors and top white and add a light bar and radios. While used for civic events and shows, this car is available for regular patrol duty on a daily basis.

1923 T-Bucket—Chula Vista, California

"Cool car!" or "I bet you could catch anything in that!" are the comments made by the young and old citizens of Chula Vista, California, when their latest "patrol" car appears.

Chula Vista's 1923 Ford T-bucket hot rod is used for community relations. It makes appearances at local events where the officers get a chance to meet and talk to the citizens. This car was acquired as a seized asset following a high-speed pursuit where drugs were found in the car. It sat, with a tarp over it, as evidence for over a year behind the fire department until the case was brought to trial and finally resolved. After the trial, the car became property of the Chula Vista Police Department.

The engine needed to be rebuilt and body work was required. The 350 Chevy engine was sent to Pete Thompson Racing Engines of Chula Vista. The four-bolt block was bored 0.040 inch over and new pistons were fitted. The crank, rods, and cam were replaced. Heads were reworked and were fitted with new valves. A B&M supercharger and Holley carb were bolted on top. The fiberglass '23 T body was lifted off the frame, cleaned up, and repainted by students at San Diego's Montgomery High School. The door was painted white (in typical black-and-white police car fashion) with the Chula Vista police logo. A roll bar was added with a light bar. Work not donated to the city was paid for from donations, usually from the officers themselves. Requests for the car's participation at local events come in at a rate of one a week. My question is, what kind of car did they use in the pursuit to catch it?

1993 FFV Taurus—Dearborn, Michigan

In May 1993, Ford Motor Company delivered forty-five 1993 Taurus Flexible Fuel Vehicles (FFV) to the Dearborn Police Department. No longer experimental, these methanol-fueled vehicles have been proven on the test track and now need some hard miles put on them in daily use. What better place to validate the safety, performance, and reliability of methanol than in vehicles driven by law-enforcement professionals?

The Dearborn Police Department has enjoyed a long and mutually beneficial working relationship with Ford. In the case of the Taurus FFV, vehicles were given for use at no cost. Dearborn is using twenty vehicles on regular patrol, with the balance of the inventory used as support vehicles. Detailed records are maintained in vehicle logbooks as to the mileage, performance, and regular maintenance of the cars. Designated vehicles oper-

ate on M85 fuel only (a mixture of 85 percent methanol and 15 percent unleaded gasoline), others use unleaded only, and a third group runs on a mixture of the two fuels. These three test groups provide engineers with data to effectively evaluate the potential environmental and economic benefits of M85 as an alternative fuel.

The Taurus FFV engine, a 3.0 liter V-6, delivers 140 horsepower with gasoline and 154 horsepower with M85. It can be fueled with M85, unleaded gas or a combination of both. The fuel sensor measures the percentage of methanol in the single fuel tank and signals the engine computer. The computer adjusts spark timing and fuel flow depending on the ratio between methanol and gasoline. Special electronic dashboard instrumentation for FFV operation shows the percentage of methanol in the fuel mixture and the driving distance to empty. The corrosive properties of methanol require special

With a wisp of tire smoke off the rear tires, a San Bernardino County Sheriff's Department Infinity Q45 lets it all hang out while fulfilling its role as a rabbit on the EVOC course.

San Bernardino's black 300ZX 2+2 rests while its pursuers wait in the background for another chance to chase it.

Left
The reflective gold graphics on San Bernardino's 300ZX blend at the same angle as the A-pillar. The horizontal stripes make the car look even longer and lower.

nickel-plated, stainless steel or methanol-compatible parts for tanks and hoses.

The Taurus FFV pictured is not a standard police package, but every heavy-duty option was added to help withstand the rigors of police patrol.

1985 LTD—Tijuana, Mexico

Police cars reaching the end of their service life as patrol cars are called "turn-outs." They may be sold or re-assigned to another form of duty within the department. They may be purchased by an individual for personal use. Some are even back on the streets as taxis. Another department looking for a low-cost patrol car may buy them. There are several police-car brokers across the country who will repair and repaint the cars and re-sell them to another department, usually with a

limited warranty. Such is the case with this attractive dark-brown-over-tan 1985 Ford LTD sedan, currently being used by the Mexican Department of Public Safety. It had served with distinction in a police department somewhere in the United States. Not yet ready for the crusher or taxi service, it was exported to Mexico. It is powered by a 3.8 liter V-6 with an automatic transmission. It is fully outfitted with light bar, siren, and police radios. Its usual duty is patrolling the highways of the city, policing commercial carriers.

1990 Ford—California Highway Patrol SMPV

SMPV stands for Specially Marked Patrol Vehicle. A program introduced by CHP in 1987, its goal was to reduce the amount of truck-involved fatal accidents. The plan was to see if truck drivers would comply more often with traffic laws if officers were in less recognizable vehicles. A pilot program was initiated, and fifteen SMPV cars were ordered. The vehicles purchased were standard police-package Ford and Chevy sedans. Instead of the traditional CHP black and white, they were every other possible color. Only the doors were painted white in the standard CHP style. Light bars, whip antennas, and spotlights were not installed. Smaller, low-profile push bars were installed in front. A red emergency flasher was installed behind the inside rear-view mirror, and emergency flashers were installed on the package tray. The initial fifteen SMPVs were deployed for one year in areas with unusually high rates of truck-involved fatalities. The program proved to be very effective. In the first year, truck-

The Arizona Highway Patrol's 1991 Thunderbird Super Coupe on loan to the department from Ford Motor Company to test hot-weather durability of the supercharged V-6. In addition to the Department of Public Safety shield on the door, it is marked as a "test vehicle" to address citizen concerns about the state of Arizona spending money on this type of car.

related fatal accidents dropped 33 percent. The success of the program led the CHP to assign eighty-six SMPVs on the road by the end of 1991.

From one successful program to another, this particular SMPV has been reassigned to the CHP's new Commercial Operator Narcotic Enforcement Team (CONET) program. The goal of CONET is to intercept shipments of controlled substances transported illegally by commercial carriers. There are fifteen teams deployed on California's interstate highways. Each team is made up of a sergeant, two traffic officers, and a dog. In 1992, the CHP intercepted drugs with a street value of almost $40 million. These interceptions were made by routine officer patrols and CONET program investigations. The CONET cars carry the usual assortment of trunk items with some interesting additions. They carry a large wooden stick almost the size of a small baseball bat. It is used to "thump" tires. A well-placed blow on a fully

Left
Without spotlights and with a light bar that blends so well into the roofline, this T-Bird Super Coupe is almost stealthy. In addition to the original factory tint, the windows of the Arizona Highway Patrol cars receive an extra dark tint to keep out the hot desert sun.

The Arizona Highway Patrol's Thunderbird Super Coupe at speed across the desert.

Large rear tires dominate the rear view of this police car. "Chula Vista Police" is prominently displayed on the tailgate of their newest cruiser.

inflated tire has a "ring" all its own. A tire used to carry something other than air will have a dull sound to it. A long thin stick is used to probe into hay bales or check fuel tanks for a false bottom. A drug-testing kit is carried to test suspected contraband. A tool kit is carried to unbolt panels or com-

ponents. Since officers must crawl under trucks, a set of wheel chocks large enough for an airliner is part of the trunk equipment. While these "stealth" cars are assigned to commercial truck enforcement, they can stop and cite other violators as well.

1977 Corvette—Jackson, Michigan

Crime Awareness Officer Joe Hankis may be the luckiest cop on the Jackson police force. About two dozen times a year, he drives a police car at community festivals, school visits and parades. Only this car is not your standard black-and-white Caprice; it's a 1977 Corvette Stingray made over into a fully equipped patrol car.

Located in semi-rural, south-central Michigan, the city of Jackson (pop. 40,000) offers a comfortable lifestyle without the hustle of a big city. But it also has the distractions that every child faces in today's changing society. The enticing 'Vette is an icebreaker that quickly melts any wariness of police officers. Usually, a kid spies the car and starts grilling Officer Hankis about its details. Before long, the conversation drifts from the car to notions of staying in school, staying off drugs, and other challenges of growing up. With a little luck, the department has made another friend and may have recruited a future officer.

This vehicle, a symbol of the department's Crime Awareness Program, cost practically nothing. The department received the car in 1989 from a drug seizure. A local service club paid for the radio equipment, including speakers behind the grill, concealed microphones, and voice-activated "Nightrider" lights mounted atop the dash. The speakers can broadcast from the mikes or from the standard police radio, and the lights flash in synch with the audio. The local Chevrolet dealer repainted the car as a gift to the department. The car's vanity plate, JUSANO (Just Say No!), was suggested by a fifth grader. He won a $100 US savings bond in a contest sponsored by the department.

*A small-block Chevy engine with a supercharger and
chrome pipes are the powerplant for this '23 T-bucket.
It is probably the only police car that can do wheelies.*

Attractive blue graphics blend well with the Taurus styling. The small "FFV" on the door and deck lid are *the only external clues that this car runs on an alternative fuel.*

The distinctive Ohio State Highway Patrol "flying wheel" logo partially covers the IROC-Z door graphics. This car is one of three red Camaros recently added to the Ohio State Patrol's fleet. All were *assembled from stolen parts and were confiscated through auto-title fraud investigations. Ohio State Highway Patrol*

One of the few CHP Specially Marked Patrol Vehicles still in service. Originally part of a successful program to reduce truck-related fatal accidents, this unit is now part of an anti-drug program. Its stealthy appearance is due to light metallic blue paint and to the absence of light bars and spotlights. Standard CHP shield on the white door makes this SMPV identifiable from the side as a CHP vehicle.

Previous pages
Performance is not lacking in Dearborn's Taurus FFV.
When running on higher percentages of methanol, the
3.0 liter engine produces more horsepower than when
running on unleaded gas.

This is the view the commercial carrier has in his
mirrors of the CHP's SMPV Ford sedan. The front
bumper has smaller than standard push bars. The only
forward-facing emergency light is a red one behind the
inside rear-view mirror. The package tray has three
rear-facing emergency lights, one each in red, blue,
and yellow.

Commonly called a "turn-out" by our departments, this attractive 1985 LTD sedan has just begun a new life south of the border with the Mexican Department of Public Safety.

An attractive paint scheme of dark brown metallic over tan graces this previously retired 1985 Ford LTD sedan. It once had an antenna mounted on the deck lid. That hole has been plugged and a new antenna relocated to the quarter panel. With a new light bar and radio, this LTD is back on patrol again.

Jackson, Michigan's crime awareness education car is a 1977 Corvette. A local fifth-grade student won a $100 US savings bond for suggesting the vanity plate (JUst SAy NO) in a contest sponsored by the department. Mickey Kress

The very attractive paint on Jackson's Corvette was a donation from a local Chevy dealer. The color scheme is the same as Jackson's regular patrol cars. Mickey Kress

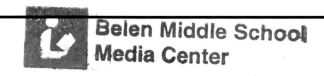
Index